Profiles of the Presidents

WILLIAM HOWARD TAFT

★ ★ ★

Profiles of the Presidents

WILLIAM
HOWARD TAFT

by Michael Burgan

Content Adviser: Harry Rubenstein, Curator of Political History Collections, National Museum of American History, Smithsonian Institution

Reading Adviser: Dr. Linda D. Labbo, Department of Reading Education, College of Education, The University of Georgia

COMPASS POINT BOOKS ✦ MINNEAPOLIS, MINNESOTA

Compass Point Books
3109 West 50th Street, #115
Minneapolis, MN 55410

Visit Compass Point Books on the Internet at *www.compasspointbooks.com*
or e-mail your request to *custserv@compasspointbooks.com*

Photographs ©: White House Collection, Courtesy White House Historical Association (120), cover, 3; Library of Congress, 7, 17, 23, 27, 28, 44; Courtesy of Army Art Collection, U.S. Army Center of Military History, 8; National Park Service, William Howard Taft National Historic Site, 9, 10, 14, 54 (top), 55 (left), 56 (left); Bettmann/Corbis, 11, 16, 18, 19, 24, 35, 40, 48, 49, 59 (bottom left); From "Illustrated Cincinnati: Pictorial Hand-Book of the Queen City" by D.J. Kenny, published in Cincinnati by Robert Clarke & Co., 1875, Photo Courtesy of the Eugene H. Maly Library, Athenaeum of Ohio, Cincinnati, Ohio, 12; Hulton/Archive by Getty Images, 13, 15 (top), 21, 32, 34, 36, 38, 41, 45, 56 (right, all), 57 (all), 58 (all), 59 (top right); North Wind Picture Archives, 15 (bottom), 22, 26, 31; DVIC/NARA, 20; Stock Montage, 25; PEMCO – Webster & Stevens Collection/Museum of History & Industry, Seattle/Corbis, 29; Corbis, 33, 37, 39; Robert Holmes/Corbis, 42; Underwood & Underwood/Corbis, 46, 47, 59 (top left); James P. Rowan, 50; Union Pacific Museum Collection, 54 (bottom); Denver Public Library, Western History Collection, 55 (right); E.O. Hoppé/Corbis, 59 (bottom right).

Editors: E. Russell Primm, Emily J. Dolbear, Melissa McDaniel, and Catherine Neitge
Photo Researcher: Svetlana Zhurkina
Photo Selector: Linda S. Koutris
Designer/Page Production: The Design Lab/Les Tranby
Cartographer: XNR Productions, Inc.

Library of Congress Cataloging-in-Publication Data
Burgan, Michael.
   William Howard Taft / by Michael Burgan.
      p. cm. — (Profiles of the presidents)
Summary: A biography of the twenty-seventh president of the United States, discussing his personal life, education, and political career.
Includes bibliographical references (p.) and index.
   ISBN 0-7565-0273-X (alk. paper)
   1. Taft, William H. (William Howard), 1857–1930—Juvenile literature. 2. Presidents—United States—Biography—Juvenile literature. [1. Taft, William H. (William Howard), 1857–1930. 2. Presidents.] I. Title. II. Series.
   E762 .B865 2003
   973.91'2'092—dc21   2002153565

j Biography
Taft

Table of Contents

★ ★ ★

*NOTE: In this book, words that are defined in the glossary are in **bold** the first time they appear in the text.*

An Unhappy President

★   ★   ★

Some politicians dream of becoming president of the United States and living in the White House. William Howard Taft had a different goal: He wanted to become the chief justice of the U.S. Supreme Court—the most important judge in the country. Other people, however, thought Taft would make a good president. They urged him to run for that office. By the end of his career, Taft had accomplished both goals. He remains the only American to have been both president and chief justice.

Taft was not a popular president, but he was a warm and generous man. Even people who did not agree with his policies saw that he was a decent person. However, Taft had trouble making important decisions, and he never felt comfortable leading the nation. He called the presidency "the lonesomest place in the world."

◄ William Howard
Taft in 1908,
the year he was
elected president

"Big Bill" Becomes a Lawyer

★ ★ ★

In some ways, William Howard Taft was well prepared for a life in the law and government. His father, Alphonso Taft, was a lawyer in Cincinnati, Ohio. Alphonso Taft

Alphonso Taft ▼

also served as a top adviser to President Ulysses S. Grant and as U.S. **ambassador** to Russia and Austria-Hungary. At that time, Austria-Hungary was a major European nation. Its lands included what are now Austria, Hungary, the Czech Republic, Slovakia, Croatia, and parts of Italy.

William was born in Cincinnati on September 15, 1857. As a boy, he was overweight. He was known as Big Lub and later as Big Bill. Despite his size, William was an active child and a good athlete.

Louisa Taft

Both of his parents wanted William to do well. His mother, Louisa, pushed him especially hard. William was the favorite of her five children. Louisa Taft led an active life, taking part in many local clubs and starting a kindergarten. Alphonso Taft encouraged his wife to have interests outside the family. William shared his father's attitude about women. When he graduated from high school in 1874, he spoke in favor of letting women vote—a legal right they did not gain everywhere in the United States until 1920.

Taft (standing in the center of the doorway) with classmates at Yale University in 1878

After high school, Taft went away to college at Yale University in Connecticut, where he worked hard to get good grades. He finished second in his class and then returned to Cincinnati to study law. In 1880, he passed the exam that made him a lawyer. After working briefly as a reporter, he became an attorney for the city of Cincinnati. In the next few years, Taft would be appointed to other government jobs in Ohio.

During his early years as a lawyer, Taft dated a young woman named Nellie Herron. In 1886, they married. Like Taft's mother, Herron was an intelligent, independent woman. She also expected Taft to succeed. Her goal was to be the first lady. As a teenager, she had once visited the White House. Her father was a friend of President Rutherford B. Hayes. After that visit, Herron insisted that whomever she married had to be "destined to be president of the United States." Throughout their marriage, Nellie Herron Taft made sure her husband sought that goal.

▲ Nellie Herron was determined to become first lady of the United States.

Road to Success

★ ★ ★

Through their families, Taft and his wife knew many powerful people in Ohio. They helped Taft get some of his jobs. In 1887, he was appointed to finish the term of a judge on the Ohio Superior Court. The next year, Taft was elected to serve a complete term on the court. It was the only time Taft ran for office until he ran for president twenty years later.

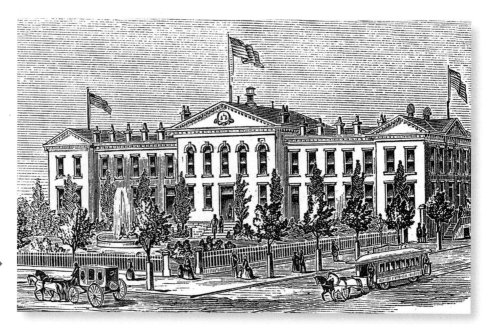

Cincinnati, Ohio, ▶
in the late 1800s

In 1889, Taft began to act on his dream of reaching the Supreme Court. He asked the governor of Ohio to bring up the subject to President Benjamin Harrison—another native Ohioan. The president thought Taft was too young to sit on the nation's highest court. Instead, Harrison made Taft solicitor general, which was another important legal position, in 1890. As solicitor general, Taft would represent the U.S. government in cases heard by the Supreme Court.

▲ *President Benjamin Harrison appointed Taft solicitor general.*

At first, Taft felt overwhelmed by his new job in Washington, D.C. Nellie, however, welcomed the chance to move to the capital so her husband could boost his career. Taft had always had a hard time speak-

Taft during his years ▲
as a judge on the
Sixth U.S. Circuit
Court of Appeals

ing in public, and be-
ing solicitor general
was not easy for him.
He soon thought
about becoming a
judge again. In 1892,
a position opened on
the Sixth U.S. Circuit
Court of Appeals,
which was based in
Cincinnati. President
Harrison agreed to
name him to the court.

For the next eight years, Taft sat on the circuit
court. He also spent several years teaching law. As a
judge, he often heard cases that involved large companies and their workers. In many cases, Taft sided with
the workers. He said workers could form unions, which
are groups that try to help workers win better pay. He
also said workers could strike, or refuse to work, as
a protest against low pay or bad working conditions.
However, Taft also supported the use of force against
workers if strikes turned violent.

In 1894, workers at the Pullman factory near Chicago went on strike. Pullman was the leading maker of sleeping cars for trains. Taft wrote his wife that the military would have to kill some of the workers to squash the strike. "They have only killed six . . . as yet," Taft wrote. "This is hardly enough to make an impression."

When ❧ ❧ ❧ ❧

You Buy a Hat,
See that it contains the Union Label.

You Buy Shoes,
See that they contain the Union Label.

You Buy Clothes,
See that they are union made

You Buy Coal,
See that it is not dug by Scabs.

YOU BUY MEAT,
See that the Packers are not antagonizing labor.

YOU BUY BREAD,
See that it is Union made.

YOU BUY ANYTHING,
See that it is not scab or penitentiary products.

Then . ❧ . .

You will be patronizing the honest union workingman and assisting the cause of humanity.

Read the "Don't Patronize" List published in all Union Labor Papers.

▲ This poster issued by the Missouri State Federation of Labor in 1895 encouraged the public to buy union made goods. As a judge, Taft often sided with unions.

◄ Illinois National Guardsmen fire on Pullman workers on strike in Chicago in 1894.

Taft had met many powerful people during his years in Washington, D.C., and he stayed in contact with them. One good friend from that time was Theodore Roosevelt. By 1897, Roosevelt was serving as president of the New York City Board of Police Commissioners. Roosevelt wanted to return to Washington, however, and he asked Taft for help getting a job there. The president, William McKinley, was from Ohio, and Taft asked him to find a position for Roosevelt. McKinley named Roosevelt assistant secretary of the navy. This favor strengthened the bond between Taft and Roosevelt.

William McKinley ▼ was the twenty-fifth president of the United States.

In 1900, McKinley asked Taft to take on a new job. The United States had won the Spanish-American War (1898). As a result of the war, Spain sold the Philippines, a group of

U.S. Philippine
commissioners
General Luke E.
Wright (left) and
William H. Taft,
with Judge Henry C.
Ide (right) in 1901

islands in the Pacific Ocean, to the United States. The
president wanted Taft to serve as the U.S. governor of the
islands. Taft did not want the job. Like many Americans,
he did not think the United States should control the
governments of distant countries. He also did not want
to leave the circuit court. Nellie, however, welcomed the
chance to go abroad. Taft finally agreed to take the job
after McKinley promised to appoint Taft to the Supreme
Court as soon as he could.

The Philippines was in upheaval when Taft arrived. Many **Filipinos** did not want their homeland to be ruled by the United States. Brutal fighting broke out between Filipino rebels and the 70,000 U.S. troops based in the Philippines. General Arthur MacArthur, the U.S. military governor in the Philippines, was not eager to give control of the islands to Taft. However, soon after the rebels' leader was captured in March 1901, Taft was sworn in as the new governor.

General Emilio ▾ Aguinaldo and his army were opposed to U.S. rule in the Philippines.

As governor, Taft had to create a new government in the Philippines based on U.S. laws and customs. He wrote a **constitution** much like the U.S. Constitution and created a court system. He also set up a public school system that taught lessons in English. Many Filipinos were poor, and Taft worked out a deal that let some of them own land for the first time. He arranged for the U.S. government to buy land that belonged to the Roman Catholic Church. Then he helped the Filipinos buy that land at a low price.

▲ *While in the Philippines, Taft established public schools like the one these children attended in 1913.*

The Tafts, including their three children, lived well in a large house in the Philippines. They had, as Nellie Taft wrote, "dear knows how many servants." Taft liked the Filipinos, and they thought he was a much better leader than MacArthur had been. Taft felt a sense of duty toward the Filipinos. He wanted to help them as much as he could. Still, like most Americans at that time, he did not think the Filipinos were ready to govern

General Arthur ▼ MacArthur (second from left) with his staff in the Philippines in 1898

◀ Theodore Roosevelt became the twenty-sixth president of the United States after the assassination of William McKinley.

themselves. Taft believed that the United States had to first teach them how to run a fair and open government. He was so committed to helping the Filipinos that he turned down two chances to serve on the Supreme Court.

Those offers to join the Court came from Theodore Roosevelt, who had been elected vice president in 1900. Roosevelt took over as president when President McKinley was shot and killed in 1901. Roosevelt finally lured Taft back to the United States with the offer of another job—secretary of war.

Presidential Friendship

★ ★ ★

At first, Taft was not sure he wanted the new job. As secretary of war, he would be the president's top adviser on military matters. Taft thought he had "no particular [skill] for managing the army." Roosevelt, however, planned to play a large role in directing the country's military forces. He also promised Taft that he would still have a hand in governing the Philippines.

Taft became ▶ Roosevelt's secretary of war in 1904.

When Taft became secretary of war in 1904, his

Taft (left) observing work on the Panama Canal in 1907

friendship with Roosevelt deepened. Roosevelt sent him on special assignments that were often overseas. Taft helped direct the construction of the Panama Canal. This water route across the Central American nation of Panama linked the Atlantic and Pacific Oceans. Taft also traveled to Japan to smooth relations with that Asian nation. In 1906, he traveled to Cuba to help end a **revolution** there and to set up a new government.

Taft was loyal to President Roosevelt's policies, and Roosevelt valued Taft's friendship. In 1904, Roosevelt was elected president. At that time, he said he would not run again in 1908. As the next election approached, Roosevelt wanted a Republican presidential **candidate** who would continue his policies, and Taft seemed like the best choice.

Taft giving a speech ▼ in Wisconsin during his campaign for president in 1908

Nellie Taft shared Roosevelt's view, and together they convinced Taft to run. Nellie played an active role in shaping her husband's **campaign** for the presidency. She gave Taft advice on how to improve his speeches. Taft, however, did not truly want to run for president. He told one friend, "I very much enjoy being in the cabinet, and shall be quite content if the **nomination** goes elsewhere." Taft often told people he was not a serious candidate—something his wife hated to hear.

▲ *William Howard Taft receiving the news from Theodore Roosevelt that he had won the Republican nomination for president*

In June 1908, the Republicans met to choose their presidential candidate. Some still wanted Roosevelt, but he had made a promise not to run. Instead, he did all he could to make sure Taft was the party's choice.

When Taft accepted the nomination, he praised Roosevelt. As the campaign went on, some people began to think Taft was running only to please Roosevelt. One reporter suggested that the letters in Taft's name stood for "Taking Advice from Theodore."

The Democratic candidate for president was William Jennings Bryan. He had run for president twice before, losing to William McKinley both times. Bryan thought the government should do more to help average citizens instead of protecting the interests of large companies. He also opposed the U.S. role in the Philippines. The question he asked voters in 1908 was, "Shall the people rule?" His answer was yes. The Republicans, he claimed, would hurt the interests of the common people.

However, many Republicans had taken steps to help the common people. At that time, politicians and social leaders called Progressives had a strong influence on the government. The

William Jennings ▾
Bryan

Progressives wanted to help average people and limit the power of big business. Theodore Roosevelt was a Progressive. If elected, Taft promised to continue his policies.

Taft hated campaigning, and at times he seemed more interested in playing golf than meeting voters. Luckily, he had Roosevelt making energetic speeches for him. Roosevelt led the attacks against Bryan and the Democrats. Bryan complained that he was running against two men, not one.

▲ *Taft playing golf in 1908, the year he was campaigning for president*

With Roosevelt's help, Taft easily won the election. After the victory, the *New York Times* said that Americans should be thankful to have such a "brave, modest, well-balanced, clean-cut citizen" as president. Taft, though, was still not sure he could do everything expected of a president. He told one crowd, "The opportunity for mistakes are so many I look forward with hesitation to the next four years."

Big Man in the White House

★ ★ ★

Taft was sworn in as the twenty-seventh U.S. president on March 4, 1909. Many of the important issues of the day involved the economy. Shortly after taking office, Taft asked Congress to pass an amendment, or change to the Constitution, that would allow the government to collect an income tax. The amendment went into effect in 1913.

Taft's inauguration ▶
in March 1909

Taft also had to deal with tariffs, which are taxes on foreign goods brought into the country. High tariffs are meant to help U.S. industries. When tariffs are high, goods made in other countries cost more in the United States. This makes people more likely to buy lower-priced American goods. However, it also raises the prices of U.S. goods because American companies can charge more for them as long as they are cheaper than foreign goods.

▲ *This harbor on Elliot Bay in Seattle, Washington, was an important site for trade during the early 1900s. Foreign goods arriving in this port would have cost more as a result of tariffs.*

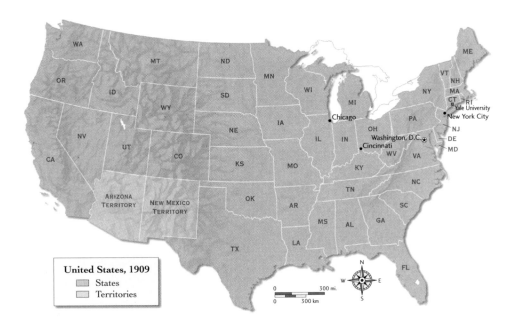

The Republican Party had long supported high tariffs, since they helped big businesses. Many Democrats and Progressives wanted to lower tariffs so prices would drop. Taft had supported lower tariffs during the campaign. In his first major action as president, he asked Congress to change the tariff. Instead of lowering the tariff, however, Congress raised it on certain goods. To keep Republicans happy, Taft went along with the new tariff. He said, "This is the best tariff bill that the Republican Party has ever passed, and therefore the best tariff bill that has been passed at all." Many people, though, did not like the higher prices that went along with higher tariffs, and they blamed Taft.

Taft was much more of a Progressive when it came to trusts, which are monopoly companies so large that smaller companies can't compete. When one large company controls an entire industry, it can charge higher prices for goods. Roosevelt had won fame as a "trustbuster." He took powerful trusts to court to have them broken up into smaller companies.

Taft also believed that it was important for companies to compete against each other. He proved to be an even bigger trustbuster than Roosevelt. Under Taft, the government started ninety legal cases against trusts. One of these broke up a trust in the sugar industry. Taft even began legal actions against U.S. Steel, the world's largest and most powerful steel company. By the end of his term, Taft slowed down his trust-busting efforts. Some Republican business owners complained that he had gone too far in breaking up large companies.

▲ *This cane-crushing machine from the early 1900s was used for sugar production. The sugar industry was controlled by a single company called a trust.*

As president, Taft focused on improving how the government was run. At that time, many government jobs were awarded based on a person's ties to the political party that held power in Washington. Taft wanted these jobs to go to the people with the best skills. He also wanted to make sure people could keep their jobs when a new party took control of Congress and the White House. Under Taft, thousands of jobs in the post office and at government shipyards were taken out of the hands of politicians.

U.S. mail vans in 1909, at about the same time Taft worked to make sure jobs in the post office weren't awarded on the basis of a candidate's political connections

▲ *President Taft signing the papers that officially made Arizona and New Mexico U.S. states in 1912.*

Taft signed two other important laws that changed the shape of the government. One called for a new amendment to the Constitution that let a state's citizens elect U.S. senators. At that time, state government chose the two U.S. senators who represented the state. Taft also signed the law that made New Mexico and Arizona states.

The U.S. Capitol ▲
in 1910

In dealing with foreign countries, Taft practiced what is called dollar diplomacy. He hoped that if U.S. companies spent money abroad, foreigners would be willing to have an ongoing relationship with America. People in other countries who worked for U.S. companies would also earn money to buy American goods. That way, Taft would be substituting "dollars for bullets" in his efforts to strengthen U.S. interests overseas.

Taft was also ready to send U.S. troops abroad if American interests seemed threatened. In 1911, he sent 20,000 U.S. troops to the Mexican border. Mexico was in the middle of a revolution. Taft wanted to let the Mexicans know that he would act if their government did not protect Americans living there. The next year,

750 U.S. Marines landed in the Dominican Republic, a nation in the Caribbean. For several years, fighting there had been hurting U.S. companies. The marines helped restore order to the country. Taft used the marines again in 1912. He sent several thousand to Nicaragua, a nation in Central America that was in the middle of a violent political crisis. The marines protected Americans and U.S. businesses in Nicaragua. For a time, they also controlled all the major cities in the country.

▼ *Marines on horseback enter the town of Chinenbega, Nicaragua, in 1913*

Taft had trouble with his weight.

As president, Taft faced much criticism. Some Democrats and Progressives did not approve of dollar diplomacy and sending troops overseas. Many Americans did not think he was an effective leader. He rarely proposed new laws. Instead, it seemed as if Taft simply reacted to what Congress did.

Taft also faced problems because of his weight. He was a large man, standing a little over six feet (1.8 meters) tall and at times weighing more than 300 pounds (136 kilograms). Taft's weight moved up and down throughout his life. Some historians think he put on weight when he was under pressure. Food gave him comfort during difficult times. Taft's weight peaked while he was president. Perhaps this was a sign of the problems he faced in office. He once wrote to his wife, "Politics, when I am in it, makes me sick." People sometimes joked about his size, and it did not help his image when he got stuck in the White House bathtub. Six men had to come pull him out. The old tub was soon replaced with a much larger one.

On the Way Out

★ ★ ★

At first, Taft could rely on Roosevelt for support and advice during tough times. As Taft's term went on, however, his actions sometimes angered Roosevelt. Taft paid more attention to **conservatives** in the Republican Party than Roosevelt had. These Republicans did not like many Progressive policies.

Taft was not as great a defender of the environment as Roosevelt had been while president. Taft chose Richard Ballinger as his secretary of the interior, the official in charge of **public lands.** Taft and Ballinger thought private companies should be able to use more public lands. These companies would make money on the land by cutting down trees and mining.

▲ Richard A. Ballinger was Taft's secretary of the interior and was in favor of allowing private companies to use more public lands.

Gifford Pinchot disagreed with Taft and Ballinger over how public land should be used.

As president, Roosevelt had worked hard to stop private companies from cutting down trees on public lands. He had put his good friend Gifford Pinchot in charge of the government's forests. Pinchot kept this job when Taft took office, but was soon arguing with Ballinger over Taft's policies on public lands. Taft backed Ballinger in the dispute, and he fired Pinchot in 1910. This angered Roosevelt and other Progressives. Taft complained that he was tired "of hearing from [Roosevelt's] friends that I am not carrying out his policies."

Over the next year, Taft made other decisions that angered Roosevelt. The one that may have ended their friendship came in 1911, when Taft tried to break up U.S. Steel. Officials working for Taft questioned Roosevelt's earlier approval of a deal by U.S. Steel to buy a smaller company. Some people thought that Taft's case against U.S. Steel betrayed an agreement that Roosevelt had made with the giant steel company.

Many people—including Taft—believed Roosevelt would run for president in 1912. Roosevelt announced he was a candidate in February 1912. By then, he had already crossed the country, giving speeches in favor of Progressive policies. Taft considered not running for reelection, but he decided to accept Roosevelt's challenge. He thought Roosevelt's Progressive ideas were "a great danger and menace to the country."

◄ *Former president Theodore Roosevelt speaking to a crowd in New Jersey during his 1912 campaign for president*

In June, the Republicans met to choose their candidate. Taft won the nomination, so Roosevelt decided to form his own party, called the Progressive Party. The new party was also known as the Bull Moose Party because Roosevelt had once said, "I am as strong as a bull moose." The third candidate was Democrat Woodrow Wilson, the governor of New Jersey. Taft was disappointed to see Roosevelt run. He knew he was not popular enough to win a three-way race. He wrote, "If I cannot win, I hope Wilson will."

A 1912 campaign ▶ banner for Roosevelt and the Progressive Party

◂ *Taft (right) with
Woodrow Wilson at
Wilson's swearing-in
ceremony in
March 1913*

Taft got his wish. That November, Wilson won the
presidency. Taft came in third—the worst finish ever for
a president seeking reelection. Despite the loss, he was
not sorry to be leaving the White House. As Taft prepared to go, he told friends, "The truth is I am glad that
it is all over."

After the White House

★ ★ ★

William and Nellie Taft soon settled in New Haven, Connecticut. Taft accepted a job teaching at Yale Law School and also wrote a series of books on government

Present-day Yale ▾ University in New Haven, Connecticut

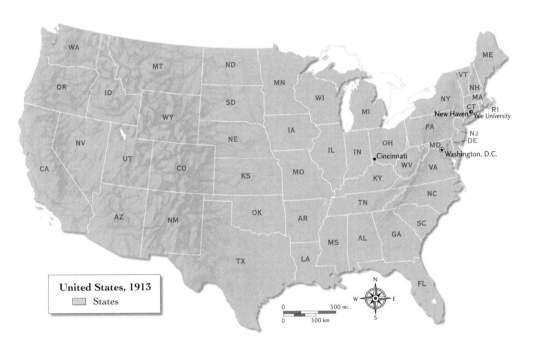

United States, 1913
States

and law. In one of these books, he questioned the aim of the Progressives. Government could correct some problems, he wrote, but "there is a line beyond which Government cannot go with any good practical results . . . to make men and society better." Taft thought Roosevelt and the Progressives had crossed that line. As he had shown during his presidency, Taft was more conservative than his old friend.

At Yale, Taft still dreamed about becoming chief justice of the Supreme Court. His chances improved in 1920, when Warren G. Harding was elected president. Like Taft, Harding was a Republican and an Ohioan. Soon after he took office, Harding told Taft he would name him to the Supreme Court when the opportunity arose. Just a few months later, in June 1921, Chief Justice Edward White died, and Harding

*Chief Justice ▶
Edward White died
in June 1921, and
Taft took his place
on the U.S.
Supreme Court.*

kept his promise. Taft was thrilled. He described being named chief justice as "the crowning joy and honor" of his life.

Taft poured all his energy into his new job. His legal views were usually conservative, and he generally supported the rights of business owners to do as they pleased. In one case, Taft refused to let Congress place a tax on goods made by child workers. Congress had hoped that fewer companies would hire children if the goods they produced were more expensive.

▲ *A child worker in a textile factory in 1910*

Chief Justice Taft ▶ (third from left) and the associate justices look at the model for the new Supreme Court building in May 1929.

As chief justice, Taft worked hard to make the Supreme Court run smoothly and tried to give it more control over the cases it heard. He used his good relations with lawmakers to win approval for a law that lowered the number of cases the Supreme Court was required to hear. This law let the Supreme Court choose more of its own cases. With help from Congress, Taft also won approval for a new Supreme Court building. At that time, the Supreme Court was located in the Capitol. For the first time, the Supreme Court would have its own building, which included offices for the justices. It opened in 1935.

While serving as head of the Supreme Court, Taft tried to reduce the number of dissenting opinions that justices wrote. Often, not all nine justices agree about how to rule in a case. Those who lose in the vote sometimes write a dissenting opinion, explaining why they disagree with the Court's decision. Taft believed that cutting down on dissenting opinions would make the Court's decisions stronger and help make people more likely to respect the rulings.

▾ *Chief Justice William Howard Taft with the eight associate justices of the U.S. Supreme Court*

Senator Robert Taft ▶ was more interested in politics than his father had been.

During Taft's later years, his son Robert became a lawyer. Taft encouraged his son to practice law in Cincinnati. Later, Robert Taft entered politics and eventually became a powerful U.S. senator. Unlike his father, the younger Taft enjoyed politics. He even sought the Republican nomination for president three times. Each time, however, he failed. Robert's son, Robert Jr., followed in his father's footsteps and served in the House and Senate.

Everyone who knew William Howard Taft could see he was much happier on the Supreme Court than he had ever been as president. The only thing that slowed him down was his health. In 1924, he suffered two heart attacks. Two years later, he admitted he was "older and

◄ Taft in February 1930, the last month he served on the U.S. Supreme Court

slower and . . . more confused." Still, he did not want to step down. Taft continued to serve on the Supreme Court until February 1930. He died a month later, on March 8, in his Washington home.

Today, many historians consider Taft a weak president. Taft didn't like politics, and he didn't want to be president. He was more content serving as chief justice and felt more successful during his time on the Supreme Court than he ever did in the White House.

William Howard ▸ Taft is buried in Arlington National Cemetery in Arlington, Virginia.

GLOSSARY

★ ★ ★

ambassador—the representative of a nation's government in another country

campaign—an organized effort to win an election

candidate—someone running for office in an election

conservatives—people who believe that the government should have a limited role in people's lives

constitution—a document stating the basic rules of a government

Filipinos—people from the Philippines

nomination—chosen as a candidate for office

public lands—lands belonging to the government

revolution—an armed uprising against the government

WILLIAM HOWARD TAFT'S LIFE AT A GLANCE

★ ★ ★

PERSONAL

Nickname:	Big Bill
Born:	September 15, 1857
Birthplace:	Cincinnati, Ohio
Father's name:	Alphonso Taft
Mother's name:	Louisa Maria Torrey Taft
Education:	Graduated from Yale University in 1878 and from the University of Cincinnati Law School in 1880
Wife's name:	Nellie Herron Taft (1861–1943)
Married:	June 19, 1886
Children:	Robert Alphonso Taft (1889–1953); Helen Herron Taft (1891–1987); Charles Phelps Taft (1897–1983)
Died:	March 8, 1930, in Washington, D.C.
Buried:	Arlington National Cemetery in Arlington, Virginia

PUBLIC

Occupation before presidency:	Lawyer, public official, teacher
Occupation after presidency:	Lawyer, public official, chief justice of the Supreme Court
Military service:	None
Other government positions:	Solicitor general of the United States; judge on the Sixth U.S. Circuit Court of Appeals; governor of the Philippines; secretary of war; chief justice of the U.S. Supreme Court
Political party:	Republican
Vice president:	James S. Sherman (1909–1912)
Dates in office:	March 4, 1909–March 4, 1913
Presidential opponents:	William Jennings Bryan (Democrat), 1908; Theodore Roosevelt (Progressive), Woodrow Wilson (Democrat), 1912
Number of votes (Electoral College):	7,676,320 of 14,088,614 (321 of 483), 1908; 3,486,720 of 13,901,838 (8 of 531), 1912
Writings:	*Four Aspects of Civic Duty* (1906); *The Anti-Trust and the Supreme Court* (1914); *The United States and Peace* (1914); *Our Chief Magistrate and His Powers* (1916)

William Howard Taft's Cabinet

Secretary of state:
Philander C. Knox (1909–1913)

Secretary of the treasury:
Franklin MacVeagh (1909–1913)

Secretary of war:
Jacob M. Dickinson (1909–1911)
Henry L. Stimson (1911–1913)

Attorney general:
George W. Wickersham (1909–1913)

Postmaster general:
Frank H. Hitchcock (1909–1913)

Secretary of the navy:
George von L. Meyer (1909–1913)

Secretary of the interior:
Richard A. Ballinger (1909–1911)
Walter Lowrie Fisher (1911–1913)

Secretary of agriculture:
James Wilson (1909–1913)

Secretary of commerce and labor:
Charles Nagel (1909–1913)

WILLIAM HOWARD TAFT'S LIFE AND TIMES

★ ★ ★

TAFT'S LIFE		WORLD EVENTS

September 15, Taft is born in Cincinnati, Ohio, to Alphonso and Louisa Taft (below) — 1857

1860

1858 — English scientist Charles Darwin presents his theory of evolution

1860 — Austrian composer Gustav Mahler is born in Kalischt (now in Austria)

1865 — *Tristan and Isolde,* by German composer Richard Wagner, opens in Munich

Lewis Carroll writes *Alice's Adventures in Wonderland*

1868 — Louisa May Alcott publishes *Little Women*

1869 — The periodic table of elements is invented

The transcontinental railroad (left) across the United States is completed

TAFT'S LIFE

WORLD EVENTS

1870

1870   John D. Rockefeller founds the Standard Oil Company

1876   The Battle of the Little Bighorn is a victory for Native Americans defending their homes in the West against General George Custer (right)

Alexander Graham Bell uses the first telephone to speak to his assistant, Thomas Watson

Graduates from 1878
Yale University (above)

1877   German inventor Nikolaus A. Otto works on what will become the internal combustion engine for automobiles

1879   Electric lights are invented

Graduates from 1880
the University of
Cincinnati Law School

1880

Becomes an assistant 1881
prosecuting attorney
for Hamilton
County in Ohio

1881   Czar Alexander II is assassinated in Saint Petersburg, Russia

1882   Thomas Edison builds a power station

TAFT'S LIFE		WORLD EVENTS

1884   Mark Twain (below) publishes *The Adventures of Huckleberry Finn*

Becomes assistant county solicitor in Hamilton County   1885

June 19, marries Nellie Herron   1886

1886   Bombing in Haymarket Square, Chicago (below), due to labor unrest

Becomes a judge on the Ohio Superior Court   1887

Appointed solicitor general of the United States   1890

1890

1891   The Roman Catholic Church publishes the encyclical *Rerum Novarum,* which supports the rights of labor

Becomes a judge on the Sixth U.S. Circuit Court of Appeals   1892

TAFT'S LIFE

Becomes dean of 1896
the University of
Cincinnati Law School

1900

Becomes governor of 1901
the Philippines

Appointed 1904
secretary of war

WORLD EVENTS

1893   Women gain voting
privileges in New Zealand,
the first country to take
such a step

1896   The Olympic Games are
held for the first time in
recent history, in Athens,
Greece (below)

1899   Isadora Duncan, one of
the founders of modern
dance, makes her debut in
Chicago

1903   Brothers Orville
and Wilbur Wright
successfully fly a powered
airplane (below)

Presidential Election Results:	Popular Votes	Electoral Votes
1908 William H. Taft	7,676,320	321
William J. Bryan	6,412,294	162

TAFT'S LIFE

Asks Congress to 1909
pass a constitutional
amendment allowing
the U.S. government
to collect an
income tax

Fires Gifford Pinchot, 1910
the nation's
chief forester

Sends troops to 1912
Nicaragua to protect
Americans there;
loses bid for reelection

Becomes a professor at 1913
Yale Law School

1910

WORLD EVENTS

1909 The National Association
for the Advancement of
Colored People (NAACP)
is founded

1913 Henry Ford begins to
use standard assembly
lines to produce
automobiles (above)

1914 Archduke Francis
Ferdinand is assassinated,
launching World War I
(1914–1918)

1916 German-born physicist
Albert Einstein publishes
his general theory of
relativity

1917 Vladimir Ilyich Lenin
and Leon Trotsky
lead Bolsheviks in a
rebellion against the
czar in Russia during
the October Revolution

TAFT'S LIFE

WORLD EVENTS

1919   World War I peace conference begins at Versailles, France

1920

1920   American women get the right to vote

Becomes chief justice of   1921
the Supreme Court (below)

1922   James Joyce publishes *Ulysses*

The tomb of Tutankhamen is discovered by British archaeologist Howard Carter

1923   French actress Sarah Bernhardt (right) dies

1926   A. A. Milne (below) publishes *Winnie the Pooh*

1929   The United States stock market collapses and severe economic depression sets in

February 3, retires from   1930
the Supreme Court

March 8, dies in
Washington, D.C.

1930

1930   Designs for the first jet engine are submitted to the Patent Office in Britain

UNDERSTANDING WILLIAM HOWARD TAFT AND HIS PRESIDENCY

★ ★ ★

IN THE LIBRARY

Casey, Jane Clark. *William Howard Taft: Twenty-Seventh President of the United States.* Danbury, Conn.: Children's Press, 1989.

Joseph, Paul. *William Taft.* Minneapolis: Abdo & Daughters, 2001.

Maupin, Melissa. *William Howard Taft: Our 27th President.* Eden Prairie, Minn.: The Child's World, 2001.

ON THE WEB

The American President—William Howard Taft
http://www.americanpresident.org/history/williamhowardtaft
For an in-depth look at Taft's life and career

Internet Public Library—William Howard Taft
http://www.ipl.org/div/potus/whtaft.html
For information about Taft's presidency
and many links to other resources

The American Presidency—William Howard Taft
http://gi.grolier.com/presidents/ea/bios/27ptaft.html
To read a biography and Taft's inaugural address

TAFT HISTORIC SITES
ACROSS THE COUNTRY

Arlington National Cemetery
Arlington, VA 22211
703/607-8052
To see where Taft is buried

William Howard Taft National Historic Site
2038 Auburn Avenue
Cincinnati, OH 45219
513/684-3262
To visit the home where Taft was born

THE U.S. PRESIDENTS
(Years in Office)

★ ★ ★

1. **George Washington**
(March 4, 1789–March 3, 1797)
2. **John Adams**
(March 4, 1797–March 3, 1801)
3. **Thomas Jefferson**
(March 4, 1801–March 3, 1809)
4. **James Madison**
(March 4, 1809–March 3, 1817)
5. **James Monroe**
(March 4, 1817–March 3, 1825)
6. **John Quincy Adams**
(March 4, 1825–March 3, 1829)
7. **Andrew Jackson**
(March 4, 1829–March 3, 1837)
8. **Martin Van Buren**
(March 4, 1837–March 3, 1841)
9. **William Henry Harrison**
(March 6, 1841–April 4, 1841)
10. **John Tyler**
(April 6, 1841–March 3, 1845)
11. **James K. Polk**
(March 4, 1845–March 3, 1849)
12. **Zachary Taylor**
(March 5, 1849–July 9, 1850)
13. **Millard Fillmore**
(July 10, 1850–March 3, 1853)
14. **Franklin Pierce**
(March 4, 1853–March 3, 1857)
15. **James Buchanan**
(March 4, 1857–March 3, 1861)
16. **Abraham Lincoln**
(March 4, 1861–April 15, 1865)
17. **Andrew Johnson**
(April 15, 1865–March 3, 1869)

18. **Ulysses S. Grant**
(March 4, 1869–March 3, 1877)
19. **Rutherford B. Hayes**
(March 4, 1877–March 3, 1881)
20. **James Garfield**
(March 4, 1881–Sept 19, 1881)
21. **Chester Arthur**
(Sept 20, 1881–March 3, 1885)
22. **Grover Cleveland**
(March 4, 1885–March 3, 1889)
23. **Benjamin Harrison**
(March 4, 1889–March 3, 1893)
24. **Grover Cleveland**
(March 4, 1893–March 3, 1897)
25. **William McKinley**
(March 4, 1897–September 14, 1901)
26. **Theodore Roosevelt**
(September 14, 1901–March 3, 1909)
27. **William Howard Taft**
(March 4, 1909–March 3, 1913)
28. **Woodrow Wilson**
(March 4, 1913–March 3, 1921)
29. **Warren G. Harding**
(March 4, 1921–August 2, 1923)
30. **Calvin Coolidge**
(August 3, 1923–March 3, 1929)
31. **Herbert Hoover**
(March 4, 1929–March 3, 1933)
32. **Franklin D. Roosevelt**
(March 4, 1933–April 12, 1945)

33. **Harry S. Truman**
(April 12, 1945–January 20, 1953)
34. **Dwight D. Eisenhower**
(January 20, 1953–January 20, 1961)
35. **John F. Kennedy**
(January 20, 1961–November 22, 1963)
36. **Lyndon B. Johnson**
(November 22, 1963–January 20, 1969)
37. **Richard M. Nixon**
(January 20, 1969–August 9, 1974)
38. **Gerald R. Ford**
(August 9, 1974–January 20, 1977)
39. **James Earl Carter**
(January 20, 1977–January 20, 1981)
40. **Ronald Reagan**
(January 20, 1981–January 20, 1989)
41. **George H. W. Bush**
(January 20, 1989–January 20, 1993)
42. **William Jefferson Clinton**
(January 20, 1993–January 20, 2001)
43. **George W. Bush**
(January 20, 2001–)

INDEX

★ ★ ★

ABOUT THE AUTHOR

Michael Burgan is a freelance writer of books for children and adults. A history graduate of the University of Connecticut, he has written more than sixty fiction and nonfiction children's books for various publishers. For adult audiences, he has written news articles, essays, and plays. Michael Burgan is a recipient of an Edpress Award and belongs to the Society of Children's Book Writers and Illustrators.